I DON'T GIVE

A

F*CK

I DON'T GIVE A F*CK

By
SHAUNDRIA MAISUN

CITIOFBOOKS, INC.
3736 Eubank NE Suite A1
Albuquerque, NM 87111-3579
www.citiofbooks.com
Hotline: 1 (877) 389-2759
Fax: 1 (505) 930-7244

Ordering Information:
Quantity Sales. Special discounts are available on quantity purchases by corporations, associations, and others. For details, contact the publisher at the address above.

Printed in the United States of America.

ISBN-13   Paperback   978-1-962366-04-5

Library of Congress Control Number: 2023916241

Shaundria Maisun
jakegomezcob@gmail.com
1107 DREXEL FORD HEIGHTS IL 60411
7089453899

CHAPTER 1

PART 1

I Don't Care: Day 1

I woke up feeling;

1.

2.

3.

Your Dream; describe in detail or what you remember,

How do you feel now?

1.

2.

3.

CHAPTER 2

Day 2

I woke up feeling;

1.

2.

3.

Your Dream; describe in detail or what you remember.

How do you feel now?

1.

2.

3.

CHAPTER 3

Day 3

I woke up feeling;

1.

2.

3.

Your Dream; describe in detail or what you remember.

How do you feel now?

1.

2.

3.

CHAPTER 4

I DON'T CARE

Day 4

I woke up feeling;

1.

2.

3.

Your Dream [in detail]

How do you feel now?

1.

2.

3.

CHAPTER 5

I DON'T CARE

Day 5

I woke up feeling;

1.

2.

3.

Your Dream [in detail]

How do you feel now?

1.

2.

3.

CHAPTER 6

I DON'T CARE

Day 6

I woke up feeling;

1.

2.

3.

Your Dream [in detail]

How do you feel now?

1.

2.

3.

CHAPTER 7

I DON'T CARE

Day 7

I woke up feeling;

1.

2.

3.

Your Dream [in detail]

How do you feel now?

1.

2.

3.

CHAPTER 8

I DON'T CARE

Day 8

I woke up feeling;

1.

2.

3.

Your Dream [in detail]

How do you feel now?

1.

2.

3.

CHAPTER 9

I DON'T CARE

Day 9

I woke up feeling;

1.

2.

3.

Your Dream [in detail]

How do you feel now?

1.

2.

3.

CHAPTER 10

I DON'T CARE

Day 9

I woke up feeling;

1.

2.

3.

Your Dream [in detail]

How do you feel now?

1.

2.

3.

CHAPTER 11

I DON'T CARE

Day 11

I woke up feeling;

1.

2.

3.

Your Dream [in detail]

How do you feel now?

1.

2.

3.

CHAPTER 12

I DON'T CARE

Day 12

I woke up feeling;

1.

2.

3.

Your Dream [in detail]

How do you feel now?

1.

2.

3.

CHAPTER 13

I DON'T CARE

Day 13

I woke up feeling;

1.

2.

3.

Your Dream [in detail]

How do you feel now?

1.

2.

3.

CHAPTER 14

I DON'T CARE

Day 14

I woke up feeling;

1.

2.

3.

Your Dream [in detail]

How do you feel now?

1.

2.

3.

CHAPTER 15

I DON'T CARE

Day 15

I woke up feeling;

1.

2.

3.

Your Dream [in detail]

How do you feel now?

1.

2.

3.

CHAPTER 16

I DON'T CARE

Day 16

I woke up feeling;

1.

2.

3.

Your Dream [in detail]

How do you feel now?

1.

2.

3.

CHAPTER 17

I DON'T CARE

Day 17

I woke up feeling;

1.

2.

3.

Your Dream [in detail]

How do you feel now?

1.

2.

3.

CHAPTER 18

I DON'T CARE

Day 18

I woke up feeling;

1.

2.

3.

Your Dream [in detail]

How do you feel now?

1.

2.

3.

CHAPTER 19

I DON'T CARE

Day 19

I woke up feeling;

1.

2.

3.

Your Dream [in detail]

How do you feel now?

1.

2.

3.

CHAPTER 20

I DON'T CARE

Day 20

I woke up feeling;

1.

2.

3.

Your Dream [in detail]

How do you feel now?

1.

2.

3.

CHAPTER 21

I DON'T CARE

Day 21

I woke up feeling;

1.

2.

3.

Your Dream [in detail]

How do you feel now?

1.

2.

3.

CHAPTER 22

I DON'T CARE

Day 22

I woke up feeling;

1.

2.

3.

Your Dream [in detail]

How do you feel now?

1.

2.

3.

CHAPTER 23

I DON'T CARE

Day 22

I woke up feeling;

1.

2.

3.

Your Dream [in detail]

How do you feel now?

1.

2.

3.

CHAPTER 24

I DON'T CARE

Day 23

I woke up feeling;

1.

2.

3.

Your Dream [in detail]

How do you feel now?

1.

2.

3.

CHAPTER 25

I DON'T CARE

Day 24

I woke up feeling;

1.

2.

3.

How do you feeeeeel now?

1.

2.

3.

I DON'T CARE

I'm hmmmmmmmmmmmm;

I woke up feeewling?

1.

2.

3.

Your Dream [in detail]

How do you feel now?

1.

2.

3.

And in conclusion:

CHAPTER 26

I'M HMMMMMMM?

Day 26

Confused, happy, sad, angry delusional, ummmmm, undecided, lost for words. This part is on you say whatever.

Your dream [in detail]

How do you feel now?

1.

2.

3.

In conclusion:

CHAPTER 27

I'M HMMMMMMM?

Day 27

I got the heck up; Now what?

1.

2.

3.

If I didn't have a dream; Oh well

How do I feel?
I do not know yet the day just started.

And in conclusion:

CHAPTER 28

WELL DANG I SLIPPED

How's it going there? You find yourself pitching thoughts around right?

Well do ya? Do ya really now? Hmmmmmmmmm,

You're not starting over this is not what this is about, find a new way "TODAY

So you woke up like this right?

How are you feeling?

In conclusion

CHAPTER 29

ANOTHER SLIP UP DANG

Enough; time to get busy SET A GAME PLAN for yourself;

Whatcha gonna do?!

1.

2.

You should start ASAP; pitch some ideas

And in conclusion;

CHAPTER 30

NO TIME TO GIVE UP: YOU JUST STARTED

So you woke feeling;

1.

2.

3.

How are you feeling now?

1.

2.

3.

CHAPTER 31

CELEBRATE YOU MADE THROUGH THE MONTH

How are you feeling now;

1.

2.

3.

In conclusion;

PART 2 AHHHHHAAAAA!

Day 1

Vent whats your plan?

How do you feel now?

PART 2 AAAAAAHHHHHAAHH!

Day 2

I woke up feeling?

1.

2.

3.

Thrown out thought:

How do you feel now?

In conclusion:

AAAAHHHAAAHHH!

Day 3

Throwing my bad thoughts for good thoughts:

How do I feel now?

1.

2.

3.

In conclusion:

CHAPTER 32

AAAAHHHHAAHHH MOMENT1

And then:

I woke up feeling like this:

And in conclusion:

CHAPTER 33

AAAHHHHHAHH MOMENT 4

And then:

I woke up feeling this way:

And in conclusion:

CHAPTER 34

AAAAHHHHHAAAHH MOMENT DAY 6

Day 6:

I woke up feeling like this;

And in conclusion:

CHAPTER 35

AAAHHHAAAAHH MOMENT DAY 7

And then:

Day 7

And in conclusion:

CHAPTER 36

AAAHHHHAAAHH MOMENT DAY 7

And Then:

Day 8

I woke up feeling this way:

So how are you doing now?

CHAPTER 37

THINGS I REEAALY WANT TO SAY/V.S WHAT I NEED TO SAY [WORK, HOME, OUT AND ABOUT ETC.]

And then:

Day 9

I woke up feeling this way:

Vent just vent.

CHAPTER 38

OOOOOHHHHH MAAAAN I____?

And then:

Day 10

I woke up feeling like this:

Do I really give a fuck?

I DON'T CARE

And then:

Day 11

I woke up feeling:

1.

2.

3.

In conclusion:

CHAPTER 39

AAAHHHHAHHHH MOMENT 12

And then:

Day 12

I woke up feeling like this:

In conclusion:

CHAPTER 40

AAAHHHHAAHH MOMENT!

And then:

Day 13

I woke feeling like this way:

Vent just VENT YA"LLLLLLLLLLL

CHAPTER 41

AAHHHHAH MOMENT

And then:

Day 14:

I woke up feeling this way:

And in conclusion:

CHAPTER 42

I DON'T CARE;

And then:

Day 15:

Do I really feel like writing today?

How I feel right now?

And in conclusion:

CHAPTER 43

I DON'T CARE

And then:

Day 16:

I woke up feeling this way:

And in conclusion:

CHAPTER 44

I DON'T CARE:

And then:

Day 17:

I woke up feeling this way:

And in conclusion:

CHAPTER 45

I DON'T CARE

And then:

Day 18:

I woke up feeling this way:

1.

2.

3.

How are you feeling right now?

AAAHHHAHH MOMENT

And then:

Day 19:

I woke up feeling this way:

1.

2.

3.

How am I feeling now?

And in conclusion:

I DONT CARE

And then:

Day 20:

I woke up feeling this way:

1.

2.

3.

How do I feel now?

CHAPTER 46

I DONT CARE

And then:

Day 21:

I woke up feeling this way:

1.

2.

3.

How am I feeling now?

I DONT CARE

And then:

Day 22

I woke up feeling like this:

1.

2.

3.

How do you feel now?

AAAAHHHA MOMENT

And then:

Day 23:

I woke up feeling this way:

1.

2.

3.

How do I feel right now?

And in conclusion:

CHAPTER 47

ANOTHER AAAHHHAH MOMENT

And then:

Day 24:

I woke up feeling this way:

1.

2.

3.

How am I feeling now?

I DONT CARE

And then:

Day 25:

I woke up feeling this way:

1.

2.

3.

How do I feel now?

And in conclusion:

I DONT CARE

And then:

Day 26:

I woke up feeling this way:

1.

2.

3.

How do I feel now?

I DON'T CARE

And then:

Day 26:

I woke up feeling this way:

1.

2.

3.

How am I feeling now?

I DONT CARE

And then:

Day 28:

I woke up feeling this way:

1.

2.

3.

How am I feeling now?

I DONT CARE

And then:

Day 28:

I woke feeling:

My Dream: How do you feel after your dream?

And in conclusion:

ANOTHER DAY

And then:

Day 29:

I woke up feeling like this:

DIDN'T SEE THAT COMING

And then:

Day 30:

And then this happened:

CHAPTER 48

DIDN'T SEE THAT COMING

And then:

Day 31:

Another day of this:

And in conclusion:

CHAPTER 49

PART 3: DIDN'T SEE THAT COMING

And then:

Day 1:

I woke up feeling like this:

1.

2.

3.

How do I feel now?

DIDN'T SEE THAT COMING

And then:

Day 3:

Not knowing what happens next:

Vent just vent:

CHAPTER 50

DIDN'T SEE THAT COMING

And then:

Day 4:

Meditate: write what you're feeling after meditation:

And in conclusion:

DIDN'T SEE THAT COMING

And then:

Day 5:

Meditations:

How do you feel now?

WOW I DIDN'T SEE THAT

And then what did you do?

   Day 6

Did you learn anything from it?

Meditate on it

WOW I DIDN'T SEE THAT

And then what did you do?

Day 7

Did you learn anything from it?

Meditate:

CHAPTER 51

WOW I DIDN'T SEE THAT

And then what did you do?

Day 6

Did you learn anything from it?

Meditate:

WOW I DIDN'T SEE THAT COMING

And then:

What did you learn from it?

Meditate:

WOW I DIDN'T SEE THAT COMING

And then what did you do?

Day 8

Did you learn anything from it?

Meditate:

WOW I DIDN'T SEE THAT COMING

And then what did you do?

Day 8

What did you learn from it?

Meditate:

CHAPTER 52

WOW I DIDN'T SEE THAT COMING

And then what did you do?

Day 9

What did you learn from it?

Meditate and reflect:

CHAPTER 53

WOW I DIDN'T SEE THAT COMING

And then what did you do?

Day 9

What did you learn from it?

Meditate and reflect:

WOW I DIDN'T SEE THAT COMING

And then what did you do?

Day 10

What did you learn from it?

Meditate and reflect

CHAPTER 54

WOW I DIDN'T SEE THAT COMING

And then what did you do?

Day 11

What did you learn from this?

Meditate and reflect:

CHAPTER 55

WOW I DIDN'T SEE THAT COMING

And then what did you do:

Day 12

And what did you do?

Meditate and reflect:

WOW I DIDN'T SEE THAT COMING

And then what did you do?

Day 13

What did you learn from it?

Meditate and reflect:

WOW I DIDN'T SEE THAT COMING

And then what did you do?

Day 14

What did you learn from it?

Meditate and reflect

WOW I DIDN'T SEE THAT COMING

And then what happened

Day 14

Did you learn anything from it?

Meditate and reflect

WOW I DIDN'T SEE THAT COMING

And then what happened after that?

Day 15

Meditate and reflect

WOW I DIDN'T SEE THAT COMING

And then what happened next

Day 15

Did you learn anything from it?

Meditate and reflect

WOW I DIDN'T SEE THAT COMING

And then what did you do next

Day 15

What did you learn from it?

Meditate and reflect

WOW I DIDN'T SEE THAT COMING

And then what did you do next?

Day 16

What did you learn from it?

Meditate and reflect

WOW I DIDN'T SEE THAT COMING

And then what happened next?

Day 17

What did you learn from it?

Meditate and reflect

WOW I DIDN'T SEE THAT COMING

And then what happened after that

Day 18

What did you learn from this?

Meditate and reflect

CHAPTER 56

WOW DIDN'T SEE THAT COMING

And then what happened next?

Day 19

What did you learn from this?

Meditate and reflect

WOW I DIDN'T SEE THAT COMING

And then what happened next?

Day 20

What did you learn from this?

Meditate and reflect

WOW I DIDN'T SEE THAT COMING

And then what happened next?

Day 21

What did you learn from this?

Meditate and reflect

WOW I DIDN'T SEE THAT COMING

And then what did you do next?

Day 22

What did you learn from this?

Meditate and reflect

WOW I DIDN'T SEE THAT COMING

And then what happened next?

Day 22

What did you learn from this?

Meditate and reflect

I DON'T CARE

And then:

Day 2

I woke up feeling like this:

1.

2.

3.

And in conclusion;

I DON'T CARE

And then:

WOW I DIDN'T SEE THAT COMING

And then what happened next?

Day 23

What did you learn from this?

Meditate and reflect

WOW I DIDN'T SEE THAT COMING

And then what happened?

Day 24

What did you learn from this?

Meditate and reflec

WOW I DIDN'T SEE THAT COMING

And then what happened:

Day 24

What did you learn from this?

Meditate and reflect:

WOW I DIDN'T SEE THAT COMING

And then what happened?

Day 26

What did you learn from this?

Meditate and reflect

WOW I DIDN'T SEE THAT COMING

And then what happened:

Day 27

What did you learn from this?

Meditate and reflect:

WOW I DIDN'T SEE THAT COMING

And then what happened?

Day 28

What did you learn from this?

Meditate and reflect:

WOW I DIDN'T SEE THAT COMING

And then what happened?

Day 28

And what did you learn from this?

Meditate and reflect:

WOW I DIDN'T SEE THAT COMING

And then what happened?

Day 29

What did you learn from this?

Meditate and reflect

WOW I DIDN'T SEE THAT COMING

And then what happened:

Day 29

What did you learn from this?

Meditate and reflect:

WOW I DIDN'T SEE THAT COMING

And then what happened:

Day 30

What did you learn from this?

Meditate and reflect:

CHAPTER 57

WOW DIDN'T SEE THAT COMING

And then what happened?

Day 31

What did you learn from this?

Meditate and reflect:

PART 4

WHAT'S NEXT

Throughout the following time what was learned?

Day 1

Meditate and reflect

WHAT'S NEXT

Throughout the following time I learned

Day 2

Reflect and meditate

WHAT'S NEXT

Throughout the following time what was learned?

Day 3

Reflect and meditate

WHAT'S NEXT

Throughout the following time what was learned?

Day 4

WHAT'S NEXT

Throughout the following time what was learned?

Day 5

Reflect and meditate

WHAT'S NEXT

Throughout the following time what was learned?

Day 6

Meditate and reflect

WHAT'S NEXT

Throughout the following time what was learned?

Day 6

Meditate and reflect

WHAT'S NEXT

Throughout the following time what was learned?

Day 8

Reflect and meditate:

WHAT'S NEXT

Throughout the following time what was learned?

Day 9

Meditate and reflect

WHAT'S NEXT

Throughout the following time I learned?

Day 10

Meditate and reflect

NOW BREATHE

Reflect

CHAPTER 58

AAAHHHHAHHH MOMENT

CHAPTER 59

I DON'T CARE

www.ingramcontent.com/pod-product-compliance
Lightning Source LLC
Chambersburg PA
CBHW071320120626
46546CB00002B/385